FEB 1 9 2002

W9-CBF-720

my
people

LANGSTON HUGHES

my people

photographs by

Charles R. Smith Jr.

ginee seo books

Atheneum Books for Young Readers

New York   London   Toronto   Sydney

The night

is
beautiful,

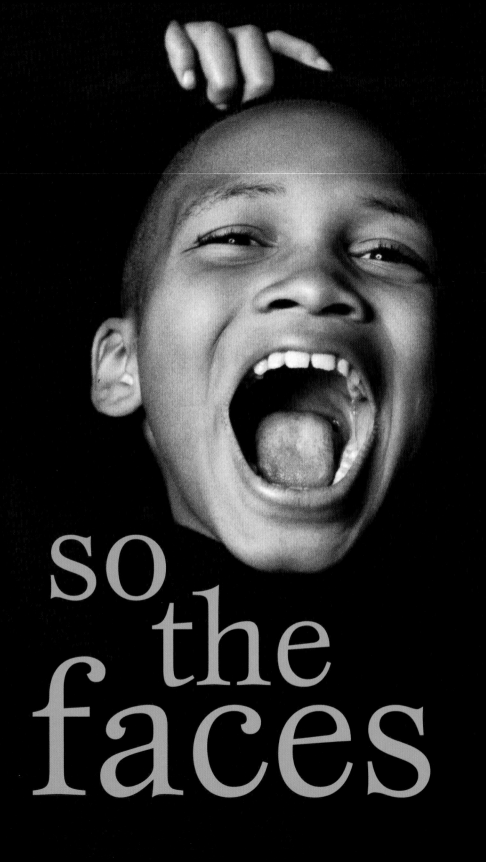

so the
faces

of
my
people.

The

stars

are
beautiful,

so
the
eyes

of
my
people.

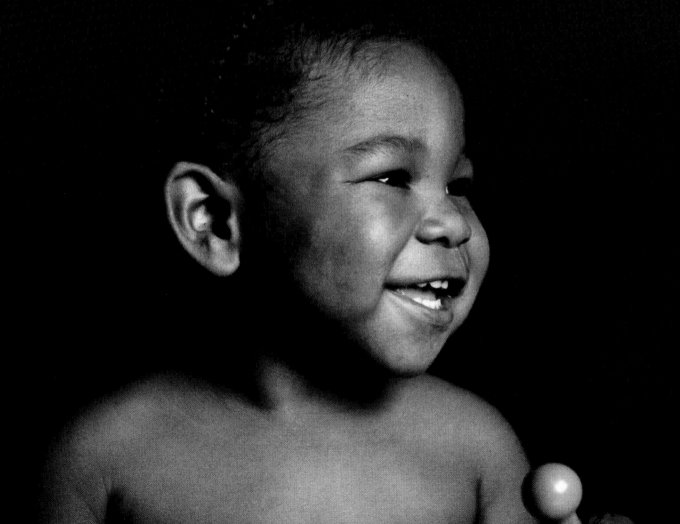

Beautiful,

also,

is the

sun.

Beautiful,
also,

are
the

souls

of my people.

Atheneum Books for Young Readers • An imprint of Simon & Schuster Children's
Publishing Division • 1230 Avenue of the Americas, New York, New York 10020 • Text
copyright © 1923 by Langston Hughes. Copyright renewed 1951 by Langston Hughes.
Reprinted from The Collected Poems of Langston Hughes. Copyright © 1994 by The Estate
of Langston Hughes. Published by arrangement with Random House, Inc., New York, NY.
Photographs copyright © 2009 by Charles R. Smith Jr. • All rights reserved, including the right
of reproduction in whole or in part in any form. • Book design by Sonia Chaghatzbanian
The text for this book is set in ITC Esprit. • Manufactured in China • First Edition
10 9 8 7 6 5 4 3 2 1 • Library of Congress Cataloging-in-Publication Data • Hughes, Langston,
1902–1967. My people / Langston Hughes ; photographs by Charles R. Smith Jr. —1st ed. • p. cm.
ISBN-13: 978-1-4169-3540-7 • ISBN-10: 1-4169-3540-1 • 1. African Americans—Poetry.
I. Smith, Charles R., 1969– ill. II. Title. • PS3515.U274M9 2009 • 811'.52—dc22 • 2008025604

To Charles R. Smith, the original,
and all of My People

—C. R. S. Jr.

Who Are "My People"?

How do you translate words into pictures?

That was the challenge when I decided to illustrate Langston Hughes's classic poem "My People."

Who should be the "people" in the book? Old? Young? Black? White? Everyone?

What should the photos look like? Serious? Playful? Head shots? Full-body shots?

These questions and more popped into my head when I thought about how I would approach the photos for this book. And to answer my questions, I looked to Langston and his eloquent words.

At just thirty-three words total, the poem is a study in simplicity, which is what attracted me to it in the first place. Langston wrote the poem to celebrate the pride he had for his black brothers and sisters in the late 1920s, when blacks were not acknowledged much in society. That helped answer one question: Only black people would be in the book, since they are who Langston celebrated. His words were not meant to dismiss other races; just to celebrate his own.

But still, who would the "people" be? To me, the words celebrate black people of differing shades and age, so I wanted to show skin color as bright as the sun and as dark as the night; I wanted to show the newness of a newborn smile and the wisdom of wrinkled skin. But, more than anything, I simply wanted to show that like any other group of people, black people come in all shapes, sizes, shades, and ages, and that each of us is unique.

—*Charles R. Smith Jr.*